Y0-DVE-064

The
Lost Colony
in
Literature

The Lost Colony in Literature

by

Robert D. Arner

Raleigh
America's Four Hundredth Anniversary Committee
North Carolina Department of Cultural Resources

1985

America's Four Hundredth Anniversary Committee

Lindsay C. Warren, Jr.
Chairman

Marc Basnight	William S. Powell	David Stick
Andy Griffith	L. Richardson Preyer	Mrs. Percy Tillett
John P. Kennedy	S. Thomas Rhodes	Charles B. Wade, Jr.
Robert V. Owens, Jr.	Harry Schiffman	Charles B. Winberry, Jr.
	Mrs. J. Emmett Winslow	

John D. Neville
Executive Director

Mrs. Marsden B. deRosset, Jr.
Assistant Director

Advisory Committee on Publications

William S. Powell
Chairman

Lindley S. Butler
Jerry C. Cashion
David Stick
Alan D. Watson

ISBN 0-86526-205-5

Copyright 1985
by the
Division of Archives and History
North Carolina Department of Cultural Resources

c. l
NC Room

For my mother and father

Contents

Illustrations

ix

Foreword

America's Four Hundredth Anniversary Committee, formed in 1978 under the provisions of an act of the North Carolina General Assembly of 1973, was charged with recommending plans for the observance of the quadricentennial of the first English attempts to explore and settle North America. The committee has proposed to carry out a variety of programs to appeal to a broad range of people. Among these is a publications program that includes a series of booklets dealing with the history of the events and people of the 1580s.

Queen Elizabeth I of England enjoyed a reign that was for the most part peaceful. It was a period of prosperity, which saw the flourishing of a new interest in literature, religion, exploration, and business. English mariners began to venture farther from home, and in time talk began to be heard of hopes to establish naval bases and colonies in America. Men of the County of Devon in the southwest of England, seafarers for generations, played leading roles in this expansion. One of these, Walter Ralegh (as he most often wrote his name), became a favorite of the queen, and on him she bestowed a variety of honors and rewards. It was he to whom she granted a charter in 1584 authorizing the discovery and occupation of lands not already held by "any Christian Prince and . . . people." Ralegh promptly sent a reconnaissance expedition to what is now North Carolina, and this was followed in due time by a colony under the leadership of Ralph Lane. Headquarters were established on Roanoke Island. After remaining for nearly a year and exploring far afield, Lane and his men returned to England in 1586.

In the summer of 1587 Governor John White and a colony of 115 men, women, and children arrived and occupied the houses and the fort left by Lane. The brief annals of this colony are recorded in a journal kept by the governor; they tell of certain problems that arose early—but they also record the birth of the first English child in America. The journal further explains why Governor White consented

xi

to return to England for supplies. His departure was the last contact with the settlers who constituted the "Lost Colony," renowned in history, literature, and folklore.

Although a casual acquaintance with the facts of these English efforts might suggest that they were failures, such was far from the case. Ralegh's expenditures of time, effort, and resources (in which he was joined by many others, including Queen Elizabeth herself) had salutary effects for England and certainly for all of present-day America. From Ralegh's initial investment in the reconnaissance voyage, as well as from the colonies, came careful descriptions of the New World and samples of its products. The people of England, indeed of the Western world, learned about North America; because books were published based on what Ralegh's men discovered, they could soon read for themselves of the natives there and the promise of strange and wonderful new resources.

From these voyages and colonizing efforts came the conviction that an English nation could be established in America. In 1606, when another charter was about to be issued for further settlement, King James, who succeeded Queen Elizabeth at her death in 1603, called for advice from some of the men who had been associated with Ralegh. They assured the king that further efforts would surely succeed. With this the Virginia Company was chartered, and it established England's first permanent settlement in America at Jamestown.

Because of Sir Walter Ralegh's vision, England persisted. Because of England's persistence and its refusal to yield to Spain's claims to the region, the United States today enjoys an English heritage. The English common law is the basis of American law; American legislative bodies are modeled on the House of Commons with the rights and freedoms that it developed over a long period of time; America's mother tongue is English, and it is the most commonly spoken language in the world—pilots and navigators on international airlines and the controllers who direct them at airports all over the world use English. Americans also share England's literary tradition: Chaucer, Beowulf, King Arthur, and Shakespeare are America's too, and Americans can enjoy Dickens and Tennyson, as well as Agatha Christie and Dorothy Sayers. America's religious freedom is also in the English tradition, and several of this nation's Protestant denominations trace their earliest history to origins in England; the Episcopal church, certainly, but the Quakers, Baptists, Congregationalists, and Universalists as well.

America's Four Hundredth Anniversary Committee has planned many programs to direct national and even international attention to the significance of events that occurred from bases established by English men, women, and children, but notably Sir Walter Ralegh, in what is now North Carolina during the period 1584-1590. While some of the programs may be regarded as fleeting and soon forgotten, the publications are intended to serve as lasting reminders of America's indebtedness to England. Books, pamphlets, and folders covering a broad range of topics have been prepared by authors on both sides of the Atlantic. These, it is anticipated, will introduce a vast new audience to the facts of America's origins.

Lindsay C. Warren, Jr., *Chairman*
America's Four Hundredth Anniversary Committee

Introduction*

Here . . . you shall finde foure of the englishe alive, left by Sr Walter Rawely which escaped from the slaughter of Powhaton of Roanocke, uppon the first arrivall of our Colonie, and live under the protection of a wiroane called Gepanacon enemy to Powhaton, by whose consent you shall never recover them, one of these were worth much labour, and if you finde them not,' yet search into this Countrey it is more probable then towards the north.

> —Instructions of the Virginia Company to
> Governor Sir Thomas Gates, May, 1609

First reported missing nearly four centuries ago, the Lost Colony of Roanoke is today as lost as ever. To be sure, almost no one since the days of Governor Sir Thomas Gates in Virginia has seriously been charged with finding out what became of it, but that does not mean that the search has been entirely abandoned. If there seems no longer any point to conducting the investigation according to the customary methods of exploration—especially since the expeditions sent out from Jamestown returned empty-handed and the ruins of the original fort at the "cittie of Ralegh" have been carefully sifted for clues — still the quest continues in a variety of other ways. In every American century, historians and then increasingly poets, playwrights, and novelists, most but not all of them southerners, have had something to say about the fate of Ralegh's missing settlers—some conjecture, plausible or (mostly) otherwise with which to make the silent American wilderness give up its secret.

What happened to the Lost Colony? How and why did it happen? And what, if anything, might Americans learn from pondering the colony's disappearance? In the attempt to answer these and other pressing questions about the nation's past, American authors have

---

*A version of this study was published as "The Romance of Roanoke: Virginia Dare and the Lost Colony in American Literature" in the *Southern Literary Journal,* 10 (Spring, 1978), 4-45. The author wishes to thank the editor of that journal, Louis D. Rubin, Jr., and the University of North Carolina Press for permission to revise and reprint the article.

presented us with one of our most attractive and enduring mythic mothers, the saintly, dispossessed, and mysterious Virginia Dare, and have elevated a footnote in colonial history to the status of a major romance worthy of taking its place next only to the story of John Smith and Pocahontas as one of the most important literary myths of American origin. As part of the "matter of early America," the romance of Roanoke is one of those tales by means of which American culture has attempted to affirm its own identity and to explain to itself the remotest sources of its ideals and aspirations, as well as some of the secret feelings of guilt and self-doubt attending the American enterprise almost from its inception.

I. "A Losse of Labor": Ralegh and the Roanoke Settlements

Up to a point, the details of the Roanoke story are as clear as convoluted Elizabethan syntax can make them. Early colonies on the coast of North Carolina, it seems, had a habit of disappearing, in one sense or another, with a frequency that would have alarmed a less dedicated man than Sir Walter Ralegh. The colony that vanished so utterly, in fact, was actually the second of Sir Walter's colonial ventures to come to nothing. The first, established in July or August, 1585, after an advance expedition led by Captains Philip Amadas and Arthur Barlowe had brought back two young Indian men, Manteo and Wanchese, and a report that declared the region to be another paradise, lasted a little less than a year. Then homesickness, a shortage of supplies, and the growing restiveness of the Indians persuaded Governor Ralph Lane to abandon the settlement and go back to England with Sir Francis Drake, whose fleet had unexpectedly looked in at Roanoke to see how the little colony was making out. About two weeks later an astonished Sir Richard Grenville, who of course knew nothing of Drake's visit, arrived with reinforcements for the deserted village. Grenville, perhaps guessing that the settlers were away on some hunting or fishing expedition, left a small garrison of some fifteen men to hold the fort. A few bleaching bones were about all that remained on Roanoke on July 22, 1587, when Governor John White came ashore with a contingent of ninety men, seventeen women, and nine children to try Sir Walter's dream once more. Understandably shaken by this mute but unequivocal testimony to the hostility of the Indians, who appear to have been provoked during an earlier visit by Sir Richard Grenville, the settlers soon sensed that they would have the same trouble with supplies if they could not depend upon the native population. What was still worse, their pilot, Simon Fernandes, had grown weary of his colonial charges and, during privateering, refused to convey the colonists to the Chesapeake Bay. Faced with such bleak prospects, the colonists prevailed upon White to return to England and see what could be done about making their future more secure.

Meanwhile, the settlement had scored two memorable firsts in the history of North American English colonization: the baptism of the Indian Manteo as a Christian and the birth of Virginia Dare, granddaughter of the governor. Virginia was the first child born to English parents in America. Born August 18, 1587, the governor's granddaughter was proudly named in honor of the new land upon which Ralegh bestowed the queen's unofficial title. But even these happy events could not raise the colonists' drooping spirits, and on August 27, just a bit more than a month after the landing, the reluctant White set sail with Simon Fernandes, leaving behind his daughter Eleanor, her husband Ananias, and their nursing infant as his private hostages to the New World.

Unfortunately for White's promise of a speedy return, he arrived in England to find a nation with little time to spare for colonial dreams. Nothing was talked of but the imminent Spanish invasion; and though the good governor attempted to keep his word, attacks by French marauders forced him back to port. By then, every available ship had been pressed into service to meet the dread Armada, and only after the defeat of that invincible fleet in 1588 could White once again think about returning to Roanoke. Even then, with Ralegh's resources rapidly being depleted, funds were hard to come by, and White had to take ship as an ordinary passenger on a West Indiaman. By the evening of August 15, 1590, White reported that the ship had come to anchor "at Hatorask"; and as the crew gazed shoreward there in the gathering twilight they "saw a great smoke rise in the Ile Roanoke neere the place where I left our Colony in the yeere 1587, which smoake put us in good hope that some of the Colony were there expecting my returne out of England."

But smoke was nearly all that White was to see. The ship's crew spent the entire next day, in fact, chasing what they took to be a second signal, only to find nothing when they arrived. The following day, after losing seven men in an unsuccessful attempt to land on the island of Roanoke, the sailors finally came ashore but discovered that the fire whose smoke they had seen two nights before had apparently started spontaneously or had been ignited by Indians or by lightning. No Englishman rushed to the beach in answer to the wilderness concert of familiar English tunes performed by the crew in order to identify themselves to any survivors, but in the sand along the ocean's edge the would-be rescuers at last came upon

4

the print of the Salvages feet of 2 or 3 sorts troaden y^t night, and as we entred up the sandy banke upon a tree, in the very browe thereof were curiously carved these faire Romane letters C R O: which letters presently we knew to signifie the place, where I should find the planters seated, according to a secret token agreed upon betweene them & me at my last departure from them, which was, that . . . they should not faile to write or carve on the trees or posts of the dores the name of the place where they should be seated. . . . [I]f they should happen to be distressed in any of those places . . . they should carve over the letters or name, a Crosse ✠ in this forme, but we found no such signe of distresse.

Still not unduly disturbed, White and his party made their way inland to the remains of the settlement proper, where they found that chests which the colonists had evidently tried to hide had been broken into and rifled. Weather-beaten books lay strewn among the weeds and wild shrubbery, their pages long since faded and illegible. One readable message remained, however: graven "in fayre Capital letters" on one of the posts of the palisade, again without any hint of distress, was the single word "CROATOAN." Overjoyed now by this "certaine token of their safe being at Croatoan, which is the place where Manteo was borne, and the Savages of the Iland our friends," White urged an immediate landing at the new place of refuge; but heavy seas thwarted the attempt. The captain having been drowned, the master soon hoisted sails for England by way of Trinidad and the Azores—over the governor's useless protests. White was later to charge that the members of the relief expedition, "regarding very smally the good of their contreymen in Virginia," had deliberately dallied in their Atlantic passage; but even if the ships had arrived before the season of storms set in, it is doubtful whether they would have learned anything at Croatoan beyond what had already been discovered on Roanoke. In 1589 Ralegh himself, perhaps anticipating the bad news White had yet to discover or deliver, penned poignant lines that may stand as the first (though certainly not the final) epitaph to Virginia Dare and the other missing colonists. "To seeke for moysture in th' Arabian sande," Ralegh pondered in Book II of *Cynthia*, "is butt a losse of labor, and of rest. . . . Seke not the Soon [sun] in clouds, when it is sett."

II. "Nothing Could We Learn": Rescue Efforts and Early Reports

With the premature departure of White's rescue fleet from North Carolina went the last remote chance of finding out what had become of Ralegh's settlers, and soon the shadows of legend and tradition began to settle and deepen around the story of the Lost Colony. The publication of White's narrative in Richard Hakluyt's *principall naviga- tions voiages and discoueries of the English nation* (1589) marks the literary debut of the romance of Roanoke, though the story had barely arrived at embryonic form and would have to wait a good long while— nearly two and a half centuries, in fact—for someone to exploit its fictional potential. Almost immediately the tale exhibited signs of a strange vitality far surpassing anything that Governor White must have imagined. As early as 1605 a windy fellow in John Marston, Ben Jonson, and George Chapman's *Eastward Hoe,* one Seagull by name, was telling everybody with the price of admission to London theaters that "a whole countrie of English" was even at that moment living comfortably in Virginia. The descendants of "those that were left there in '79," he affirmed with a cavalier disregard for chronological fact that has stuck with the romance ever since, these mythical Englishmen had "married with the Indians, . . . [who] are so in love with 'hem, that all the treasure they have they lay at their feet" (Act III, Scene ii).

Designed to spoof the extravagant tales already beginning to filter back to England from the wilds of America, Marston, Jonson, and Chapman's drama had nonetheless inadvertently set forth a theory that would persist through the centuries and, invoked by historian and romancer alike, eventually become the most popular way of accounting for the disappearance of the Lost Colony. The appeal of intermarriage, we may surmise, lies equally in the way it denies that any catastrophe to the English imperialistic enterprise ever took place and in its almost effortless gratification of the white man's ego: though we stole their land and scoffed at their religion, they could not help falling in love with us anyway.

Still, one statement does not make a myth; and despite this prom- ising beginning, it is possible that the Lost Colony might even yet have

Title page of John Marston, Ben Jonson, and George Chapman's play *Eastward Hoe. As It was playd in the Black-friers* (London, 1605).

faded from memory in a generation or so had it not been for the establishment of a permanent base at Jamestown in 1607. This development initiates what we may call the colonial phase of the romance, a span of more than a century during which hearsay and hypothesis began to shape the details of the legend, moving the story from exploration to explanation and from the broad and simple daylight of historical fact toward the twilight of romance proper. The first man to write from Virginia with additional news about the Lost Colony was no less a personage than Captain John Smith, already a controversial figure well on his way to becoming a legendary character in his own right and whose story would become progressively intertwined with that of the missing colonists as the centuries passed. But his initial remarks were prosaic enough, though tantalizing in their own way. Presumably during the days when he had been a captive of the Indians, Smith had had the chance to talk with Opechancanough, Powhatan's brother and a chief of some stature, about the Lost Colonists; and from him he learned of "a place called Ocanahonan" where, report had it, there dwelt several men who wore European-style clothing. Accompanied by a map drawn by Captain Francis Nelson, which identified the very spot where "remayneth 4 men clothed that came from Roonok to Ochanahowan," Smith's

7

story was published in his *A true relation of such occurrences and accidents of noat as hath hapned in Virginia since the first planting of that Collony* . . . (1608) and fueled anew the fires of the English imagination. The captain himself had never seen these strangely clad people, but upon his return to Jamestown he dispatched Michael Sicklemore, Nathaniel Powell, and Anas Todkill to see what they could learn about the rumor. The same Indians who had been so talkative before, however, now refused to permit an interview, and this first expedition ended with nothing more to report than the curious fact that some of the trees around the Jamestown settlement, in ironic echo of Governor White's original distress signal, bore newly carved crosses in their bark—'assured Testimonies," as one contemporary writer rather too sanguinely put it, that there were Christians alive and well somewhere out in those godforsaken woods.

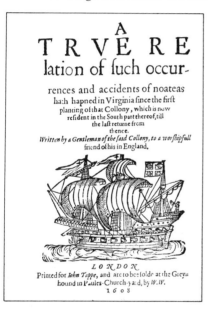

A
T R V E R E
lation of fuch occur-
rences and accidents of noateas
ha:h hapned in Virginia fince the firft
planting of that Collony , which is now
refident in the South part thereof,till
the laft returne from
thence.
Written by a Gentleman of the faid Collony, to a worfhipfull
friend of his in England.

L O N D O N
Printed for *Iohn* Tappe, and arc to be: folde at the Grey=
hound in P.aules-Church-ya:d, by *W.W.*
1 6 o 8

Title page of Captain John Smith's *A true relation of such occurrences and accidents of noat as hath hapned in Virginia since the first planting of that Collony* . . . (London: Printed for John Tappe, 1608). Photograph courtesy Rare Book Division, New York Public Library, Astor, Lenox and Tilden Foundations; reproduced with permission of the New York Public Library.

Another early writer, William Strachey, seemed to know even more about the story than Smith. In his *Historie of Travaile into Virginia Britannia,* written about 1612 but unpublished until 1849, he added another town, ''Peccarecemmek," to the one Smith had mentioned and provided as well a few intriguing architectural details. Unlike Indians who had no previous contact with European civilization, he said, the inhabitants of these two towns lived in ''houses built with stone walls, and one story above another. . . .'' So far as Strachey could see, there was only one explanation for this phenomenon: the Indians must have learned their lore from "those English who escaped the slaughter at Roanoke, at what tyme this our Colony under the conduct of Captain Newport landed within the Chesapeake Bay. . . ." If this explanation seems confused at first, Strachey meant only to say that there had very likely been two Roanoke massacres—or perhaps that the Lost Colony had flourished all the while that other Englishmen were absent from the New World—but that when the English arrived in larger numbers, Powhatan, fearing exposure of his earlier crimes, had instigated the murder of nearly all the original survivors.

Credibility in this tale is somewhat undermined by Strachey's off-handed remark that those who still live at Peccarecemmek and Ochanahowan capture "apes in the mountains" as a favorite recreation, but his really important contribution to the growing legend comes in his census of the survivors, who, he says, still live under the protection of a minor chieftain named Eyanoco. There were seven of them in all, "fower men, two boys, and one young mayde"; and although Strachey offered no more information, it would require very little imagination indeed for succeeding generations of romancers to bestow on that anonymous maiden the inevitable historical identity of Virginia Dare.

Despite the persistence of these scattered stories, however, results remained discouraging. Strachey himself professed to know much more than he had related, but for some reason, possibly because he did not think it would make any difference or perhaps because he had lost interest in the rumors, he never bothered to tell it. Captain Smith, after his brief flare-up of enthusiasm, was to estimate the chances of finding any remnants of the Lost Colony alive as very slight. For all the effort, those enigmatic crosses carved into trees—perhaps the earliest examples of Indian humor in American history—were just about all the hard evidence that ever turned up; and at last one of Smith's lieutenants, the intrepid Anas Todkill, was moved to pronounce an end to the whole endeavor with words that he must have believed would serve the missing colonists as an epitaph for all time. "Nothing could we learn," said Todkill, "but they were all dead."

But old stories never die or simply fade away. By then, at any rate, too much energy had been invested in the search to give up so easily; and for at least a century after Todkill's valediction, reports of a curiously clad and, sometimes, bearded tribe of Indians continued

9

to make their appearance in early travel literature. Thus, for example, John Lederer, a German visitor to North Carolina in the years 1669-1670, told of a powerful nation of bearded men living about two and a half days' journey from the original Roanoke settlement, and in 1704 the Reverend John Blair made note of a "very civilized" tribe of Indians who were supposed to be settled south of Albemarle Sound.

Gradually, until tradition came to possess the authority of fact, the search began to center on the Croatan Indians, a subtribe of the Hatteras family in the region of the Outer Banks, as the most likely candidates to be carrying in their veins the blood of the lost Englishmen. The last colonial writer of note to deal with the Roanoke evidence, the North Carolina historian John Lawson, argued this position most persuasively in his *New Voyage to Carolina* (1709), though he was something less than delighted by the considerations to which it lead him. Certain tribal legends among the Hatteras Indians, he claimed, "tell us, that several of their Ancestors were white People, and could talk in a Book [read], as we do; the Truth of which is confirmed by gray Eyes being found frequently amongst these *Indians,* and no others." Then Lawson, who also offers us the first evidence that the Lost Colony had passed into bona fide folklore sometime around the end of the seventeenth century by recording the "pleasant Story" that the ship that brought the colonists in the first place still appears occasionally under full sail off the Carolina coast, advances his own explanation of the mysterious silence maintained by the colonists for all those centuries. "Thro' the Treachery of the Natives . . . ," he hypothesizes, "we may reasonably suppose that the *English* were forced to cohabit with them . . . and that in the process of Time, they conform'd themselves to the Manners of their *Indian* Relations. And thus we see," he concluded darkly, "how apt Humane Nature is to degenerate."

It was a sinister twist to a familiar theory, one that left the colonists worse off than they had been before: exiled from history, outcast from their race, and permanently cut off from Christianity and the culture that should have sustained them. Englishmen no longer, the missing settlers had become an object lesson on the dehumanizing power of the American frontier, expressing in the same manner as other victims of Indian captivity a deep fear of cultural transformation. The Indian grew into a symbol of the dusky, savage inner self that, even on the threshold of the Age of Reason, Lawson had no trouble in discerning in all mankind. We hold our identities by a fragile thread indeed, he recognized; and once the continuity of memory is severed, we may easily be molded into new and anomalous creatures fitted for the population of this strange New World. From Lawson's day to our own, the swarthy specter of Roanoke would haunt the romance; and though later writers tried all sorts of ruses and evasions to deny the implications of its involvement with the story, it could be neither entirely ignored nor ritualistically exorcised.

What, then, had happened to the Lost Colony? Those writers closest in time to the event failed to provide a final answer, and more recent historians have not fared any better. Their perplexity may be indicated by the anxious queries of John Esten Cooke, who certainly knew the value of a good legend when he heard one, in his *Virginia: A History of the People* (1883): "Had the poor people wandered away into the cypress forests and been lost? Had they starved on the route to Croatoan? Had the Indians put them to death?" As will be seen, this catalog of possibilities falls far short of being exhaustive, especially once the romance had a chance to take off in earnest.

III. Archetypes of American Experience: The Romance in the Nineteenth Century

These are all the important historical sources of the Roanoke romance. Fragmented as they are, they nevertheless complement Governor White's earlier account to deepen the mystery of the Lost Colony and suggest a story rich in intrigue and high adventure. At first, however, interest in the tale remained localized and merely antiquarian, as in historian Francis X. Martin's early (1829) anecdote about "the Stump of a live oak, said to have been the tree" on which the word "CROATOAN" was carved, which he reported to have been still standing as late as 1778. Historian Joseph Seawell Jones wrote that he had "encountered two persons of very advanced years" who remembered and deplored the death of "Sir Walter's Tree," as it had come to be called, though he also affirmed that the last remains of its stump still survived (*Memorials of North Carolina*, 1838). For even the woefully unlettered inhabitants of the Outer Banks, the same historian said, such relics were ties to a legendary past of which they could be justly proud.

The attention of Americans was soon to be focused on the Lost Colony for reasons more important than mere nostalgia or antiquarianism. Early in the nineteenth century, when Americans began to cast about for materials out of which to construct a national mythology, the story of the Lost Colony was one of the first sources they discovered. This time, though, the emphasis was upon attempts to explain how the missing settlers, Englishmen no longer, had become Americans and what legacies, if any, they might have left us. It was transparently a quest for a new American parentage—in other words, a search born at least in part of the Revolutionary rhetoric of violent separation, mutilation, and disinheritance and foreshadowed by such early announcements of provisional American identity as the popular "Sons of Liberty" metaphor and the emerging claims in some areas to paternal descent through the Pilgrim Fathers. Though many of the facts around which the romance was built came straight out of colonial chronicles, the procedure for bringing the scattered details of the story together into a coherent narrative was in fact authorized by a new sort of historical methodology, the methodology of a New England historian by the name of George Bancroft.

At first glance, Bancroft's contribution to the romance of Roanoke might not appear to amount to much since he gave the story only a few pages in the first volume of his *History of the United States, from the Discovery of the American Continent* (1834). But in his preface to the first edition of that monumental work, Bancroft explained his reasons for wishing to publish the initial volume separately (and the wide popularity of that book guaranteed that his would also be the working assumptions of American historians for generations to come). "I have dwelt at considerable length on the first period," he wrote, "because it contains the germ of our institutions. The maturity of the nation is but a continuation of its youth. The spirit of the colonies demanded freedom from the beginning." From this perspective, it seemed to Bancroft that Jacksonian democracy, which was even then waging a struggle against the forces of European corruption, had been predicted and, in a measure, virtually accomplished by the farsighted Walter Ralegh and his brave band of settlers, who arrived in America with more subversive ideas than they could have guessed and who needed only exposure to the promise of the vast American continent to confirm their political antagonism to myopic Old World monarchs.

Bancroft's basic metaphor for interpreting Ralegh's entire colonial commitment was frankly epic in its implications, portraying Ralegh

Historian George Bancroft was the first writer to impart to the romance of Roanoke the notion of divine will. His interpretation of the story of the Lost Colony sparked additional literary interest in the tale as a source of national mythology. Engraving from *Dictionary of American Portraits* (New York: Dover Publications, 1967), p. 32.

13

as another Aeneas and stressing the twin themes of westerly wandering and divinely appointed destiny; and, like the *Aeneid,* his mythic historiography involved reading˙ backward in an effort to free America—as once Virgil had released imperial Rome—from the doomed cyclical pattern of the rise and fall of nations. As Robert H. Canary has succinctly summarized it, Bancroft's philosophy began with the premise that "history was the progressive unfolding of the divine will; the significant events in the past were those which pointed to the future, and his object was to construct a narrative action leading to the present." Or, as Bancroft himself put it, "the fortunes of a nation are not under the control of blind destiny . . . [but] follow the steps . . . [of] a favoring Providence."

Traces of Bancroft's interpretation of the Lost Colony continue to turn up in histories written well into the twentieth century, as, for example, in J. A. C. Chandler and T. B. Thames's allusive assertion that the colony of Roanoke must be understood as "that inevitable John the Baptist, whose voice crying in the wilderness . . . prepared the way for the coming of larger dispensation." But it is on the romance itself that Bancroft's theories had their greatest impact, even if sometimes in ways that might have baffled him. The first person to work up the story in full and proper fictional form, for instance, was a Yankee lady named Cornelia L. Tuthill, whose "Virginia Dare; or, the Colony of Roanoke" appeared in Thomas W. White's *Southern Literary Messenger* in September, 1840. Though Tuthill could not follow Bancroft all the way in his admiration for the democratic masses of the Lost Colony, she nevertheless paid explicit tribute to his *History* before turning to her tale, a story in which the star-crossed colony, betrayed and abandoned by the sailor with the suspiciously Spanish name of Simon Fernandes, finds itself assaulted by the wicked Ocracoke Indians. The settlers put up a stout defense against overwhelming odds but are losing ground steadily when they accept the offer of Manteo, the Christianized chief, to lead them away under cover of darkness to the secluded Vale of Mehezin, a more splendid paradise by far than the island of Roanoke had been.

At Mehezin they live in perfect harmony with the red man for many years, learning the forest lore that he could teach them, while Virginia blossoms into maidenhood, converts the entire tribe to Christianity by her beautiful example, is wooed by but rejects an Indian suitor named Arcana, and eventually finds true happiness in the arms of a wandering explorer from Jamestown named, of all unromantic

14

things, Henry Johnson. Virginia's bliss is short lived, however, for Henry soon dies of a wasting illness and is followed in a few months by her mother, Eleanor. Her father, inexplicably named George instead of Ananias, has been disposed of long since in the first Indian attack, leaving the young girl as the last white person prowling so deeply in the American wilderness. But if her life of loneliness seems mournful to us, Tuthill hastens to assure us that we should not judge by appearances. Virginia, she says, in a conclusion that stressed the sentimental politics of the middle class, earned in America what Queen Elizabeth could not attain in England: "the devoted affection of one true heart"; and even "Fame was not denied her,—for she was remembered among the tribe—who preserved the history of her eventful life, as the 'White Angel of Mercy.' "

With this first fictional treatment of the story, the fundamental pattern of the Roanoke romance had been set for good and all. Perhaps a better way to put it might be to say that Tuthill stumbled intuitively upon the real reason for telling the tale in the first place—our profound inability to believe that over one hundred civilized, Christianized Englishmen could possibly have been wiped out by illiterate pagans—and that she also found by an even greater stroke of luck the only narrative formula that would make sense to American readers. Here the story reminds us of what General William Tecumseh Sherman is reported to have said when news of Custer's massacre reached him in Washington—'I don't want to believe it, if I can help it'—and gets us into the processes by which the mind transforms unacceptable facts into at least minimally acceptable fictions. The Custer legend, in fact, provides illuminating parallels to the Roanoke story: a coward or a traitor or perhaps simply a fool gets a vastly outnumbered band of heroes into deep trouble; they are surprised by a sudden attack but fight courageously and to the last man if necessary, retiring in good order to the very end; and they either die with their boots on or accept the aid of some miraculous guide who at the last moment slips them past the enemy so that they may live to fight another day.

Beneath an elaborate surface of plots and subplots that may be either entertaining or embarrassing, in short, the Roanoke romance reduces to an old, old story not very different from the first book of the *Aeneid*, the Battle of Maldon, the desperate stand of Roland in the pass at Roncavilles, and even a recent movie version of the Battle of the Bulge. We are dealing here with thinly disguised heroic myth, and perhaps

15

only the historical presence of Virginia Dare, who is simply too interesting to be killed off so quickly, prevents romancers from working out the story in every detail of heroic defeat. The special American twist is that, more often than not, Virginia is the sole survivor of the catastrophe, preserved by the savages out of an uncontrollable love for her pure white beauty. But even this racial element does not measurably affect the essential structure of the plot. Retelling the story in this way enables us to snatch at least a Pyrrhic victory from the grisly jaws of defeat and to answer, at least to our own satisfaction, John Lawson's grim speculation that in this contest savagery triumphed over civilization.

As it happens, Tuthill also understood something else about Virginia Dare that subsequent romancers were to find important. Dressed in a scant white doeskin and armed with a bow and arrows, which she knows perfectly well how to use (she even accidently wounds Henry Johnson, who is hiding in the bushes, in Tuthill's version of the story), Virginia emerges from tale after tale as our American Artemis, the virgin huntress Diana; and her consort is invariably the Wild Hunter. She embodies the free spirit of the new land whose name she bears, though her devout Christianity also indicates her close ties with civilization and transforms her simultaneously into a Protestant Madonna and Virgin figure. The double allusion also suggests the difficulty authors have in locating a proper mate for Virginia, since they are as reluctant as Tuthill is to turn her over absolutely to the Indians. The striking thing about this role of the virgin huntress is the number of times, as in Tuthill's tale, Virginia wounds even her racially legitimate lovers, as if in delayed and disguised retribution for having remained so long companionless.

Even in Tuthill's rather pleasant story, then, there is something disquieting about Virginia Dare, a negative, almost threatening aspect to her personality that is difficult to define, especially in a story written by a woman writer immune, or so we would think, to castration anxieties. Perhaps the best explanation is to see Virginia as an anima figure, an image of femininity in its manifold aspects as creator, nurturer, and destroyer, and to acknowledge that both male and female writers alike may respond to the deep unconscious urge to come to terms with feminine complexity as a key to their own creative personalities. At any rate, Virginia Dare herself certainly emerges as an ambiguous symbol of the American past from Cornelia Tuthill's tale, and subsequent romances will do little to diminish that ambiguity.

Tuthill's reworking of the Roanoke materials anticipated only by a short time the South's rediscovery of its colonial past. In 1841 the Reverend Calvin Henderson Wiley, a prominent North Carolina clergyman and educator (who during the Civil War was to write a tract with the interesting title of *Scriptural Views of National Trials; or, God's Plan for the Peace and Independency of the Confederate States of America*), produced a novel entitled *Roanoke; or, "Where Is Utopia?"* The book is not primarily about the Lost Colony but rather about the famed North Carolina Regulators' rebellion of pre-Revolutionary days. As a historical metaphor, however, the rebellion mediates between the remote and the recent past, both of which are invoked in an opening encomium to the fresh, green foliage of North Carolina, which has not yet been scorched by the hot breath of the "demon of Progress."

Moving freely backward and forward in history, Wiley eventually succeeds in suggesting that the legend of the Lost Colony forms but the first episode in a continuing southern story of loss, loneliness, and alienation from history and modernity. Eventually he too succumbs to the temptation to explain what had happened at Roanoke so many years before; his hero, Walter Roanoke (alias Walter Tucker, son of Old Dan Tucker and bosom friend of Zip Coon), turns out to be a direct descendant of Manteo's daughter and Sir Walter Ralegh's son, who no less a figure than Father Time reveals did not die in the general massacre. When he makes these disclosures, Father Time leads by the hand a white-veiled, amaranthine-wreathed maiden, suggestive, of course, of Virginia Dare; and in the main line of Wiley's narrative there is another maiden, Utopia—like Virginia, she bears the name of her birthplace—who, also like Virginia, vanishes into the North Carolina wilderness when she learns that Walter, whom she loves, wishes to marry a girl named Alice Bladen.

In the final chapter, the narrator himself participates in the search for the mysterious lost Utopia, tracing her passage through the southern countryside and at last dropping all pretense that she is to be understood as anything other than a symbol of beleaguered southern gentility. "Where, where . . . is Utopia?" he anguishes. "Where is that pleasant land, and those good people of which I dreamed so much before I was wise?" That question, in one form or another, would reverberate throughout all notable southern writing of the coming century; but always the despairing answer would come back the same: look to see them no more, for theirs is a civilization gone with the wind.

Thus, the legend of the Lost Colony belongs intimately to southern history, not simply because the story happened there—that appears at times merely a strange and fortuitous coincidence—but because the South is its own Lost Colony, and ours, as Wiley seems dimly to have perceived and as he emphasized by republishing his novel in 1866, just one year after Appomattox. To the extent that the rest of the nation also subscribes to the southern story of the Lost Cause, at any rate—and the millions of people who have flocked to theaters to see *Gone With the Wind* and similar Civil War epics suggest that this is to a very great extent indeed—we acknowledge that in that tragic conflict some sort of innocence and elegance was permanently sacrificed to the forces of a disorienting modernism and that we are all somehow the poorer for its passing.

The theme of a lost innocence even an occasional nineteenth-century northern writer could appreciate, and in 1884 one of them, Hawthorne's son-in-law, George Parsons Lathrop, cast the fable of the strayed Southland into yet another Roanoke tale, a long story entitled *True*. Like Wiley, Lathrop used the Lost Colony as a historical metaphor to contrast degenerated poor whites with their heroic southern ancestors; picking up John Lawson's early reference to gray eyes as a central physiognomic symbol of that inherited identity; changing the name of Eleanor Dare to Gertrude Wylde; and creating a Yankee hero, a New Yorker named Lance, whom he introduces to a young plantation belle named Jessie Floyd in the days just after the Civil War. Lance tries to get Jessie to admit what anyone with eyes can see: that she might be distantly related to a half-breed named Adella Reefe and that to persist in denying that fact is to attempt to deny the historical interrelationships among the races in the South.

But if the South had attempted to ignore its racial realities, Lance is so obsessed by them that, in true Yankee fashion, he sees historical prototypes lurking behind every event. When he imagines that the black servants who decorate Jessie's room with flowers for her birthday are ritualistically reenacting the worship of pure whiteness, which the Indians had long ago performed in the presence of Gertrude Wylde, a story that started out to be an examination of an inherent flaw in the southern racial heritage has backed itself into the same kind of corner. Whatever Lathrop may have wished to say about how the South came to be our Lost Colony, the racial hierarchy endorsed by Lance's musings in contradiction of all his public protestations leaves us with Jessie's own utterance as the more likely of the two truths of this true story: " 'I won't have it so!' " Jessie exclaims when Lance first puts the proposition of a shared heritage to her. " 'I don't care if it is. . . . She has Indian blood; and that makes all the difference.' "

Meanwhile, the South seems to have set out to reclaim as much of its lost romanticism as possible. In 1875 a southern lady known to posterity only as Mrs. M. M. had published in the North Carolina magazine *Our Living and Our Dead* a tale entitled "The White Doe Chase," a pre-Revolutionary Indian legend, or so she claimed, about a mysterious white doe that for well over a century had haunted a lush southern woodland near the seacoast, driving out all other game. Mrs. M. M's Indian authority sounds suspiciously like William Wordsworth, author of "The White Doe of Rylstone," but her story exceeds even the tale of transformation he dreamed up. Invulnerable to ordinary shot and shell, Mrs. M. M's animal is finally ritualistically hunted down and mortally wounded by a rifle charged with mussel pearls. To the astonishment of the hunters, the stricken deer vanishes in a vapory mist, and there appears instead the wraithlike form of the long lost Virginia Dare, who spends her last hour on earth telling of the fall of Roanoke; of her strange transformation into a white doe by the magic of the good Indian Great Medicine, who wished to save her from the lustful clutches of an evil Indian called Gray Eagle; and of the impending Revolutionary War. Then, in still more somber tones, she predicts the day when brother shall turn against brother in the American Civil War, adding that she is happy to be released by death from her metamorphosed mortal form before that appalling day arrives.

Scarcely missing a beat over this dire prognosis—actually, of course, the easiest kind of prediction to make, a retrospective one—the Roanoke romance passed from Mrs. M. M's story to a more traditional one, Edward Ingle's "Roanoke: A Tale of Raleigh's Colony," which, with its publication in San Francisco's *Overland Monthly* in November, 1886, at last spread the story from sea to shining sea. Apart from a new hero named Sidney More (shades of Arcadia—or is it Utopia?) and a new villain named Jack Cage, who remains, however,

LITERARY DEPARTMENT.

———o:-:-:o———

[Written just before the war, by Mrs. M. M.]

THE WHITE DOE CHASE.

A LEGEND OF OLDEN TIMES.

CHAPTER I.

In a district of country, bordering on the Albemarle Sound there was a certain forest in which the Aboriginal hunters had luxuriated in fat venison, time out of mind. The maple tree and deer plant abounded here, and the reed swamps afforded delicious grazing for the deer, when the green herbage and foliage had disappeared at the approach of winter.

Tradition told this tale, though since the arrival of the white man this portion of the country had been entirely abandoned by the monarch of the forest, save one White Doe.

A beautiful creature she was, of snowy whiteness, exquisite form, and moving as it were upon air; her proud head erect, her dark eyes beaming with ardor, though expressive of touching sadness. As fleet as the winds—only a transient glance of her unearthly loveliness was ever enjoyed by the admiring beholder.

At the first blast of the hunter's horn, or opening of the hounds, forth she would spring from some dense coppice or entangled brake, bounding alike over fences and ditches, thickets and ravines, on the wings of the wind, she vanished from the eyes of her pursuers before they had well experienced the ardor of the chase; and back came the yelping hounds, cowering and trembling from the place of her mysterious disappearance. Such had been the fortune of every hunter in the White Doe chase since the memory of the white man; and thus for ages, this White Doe had continued to inhabit this luxuriant district, to the total exclusion of all else of the sylvan train.

"The White Doe Chase," alleged by its author, known only as Mrs. M. M., to have been a pre-Revolutionary Indian legend, was published in *Our Living and Our Dead,* a North Carolina literary magazine, in 1875. The first page of the article is shown above. From *Our Living and Our Dead,* III (December, 1875), p. 753.

suspiciously only half English, the tale adds little to the accumulating legend except the device of reporting the recovery of the story from a newly discovered notebook. Virginia Dare dies at the end of this tale, and the surviving colonists plunge once more into the American wilderness, leaving us with the original historical void that Ingle had sought to fill in the first place.

More compassionate is E. A. B. Shackelford's *Virginia Dare: A Romance of the Sixteenth Century* (1892), which for the first time arranges a marriage between Virginia and her Indian lover Iosco and even obligingly brings a Protestant minister to the Indian village in order properly to sanctify the union. Shackelford's is also the first of the Roanoke tales to turn the heroic formula underlying the story to anti-democratic advantage and implicitly challenge some of Bancroft's Jacksonian formulations.

Previous romancers, probably inspired at least in part by Bancroft's assassination of the Spanish (and, for that matter, also the French) national character and stimulated anew by the vast influx of "undesirable" immigrants into American cities, had been satisfied to blame the troubles of the Lost Colony either upon scheming Indians or, as Cornelia Tuthill had done, upon the swarthy Simon Fernandes, who stands in her story as a symbol both of Spanish intrigue and unrestrained economic self-interest. Along the same lines, Edward Ingle describes his villain, Jack Cage, as having inherited from his Italian mother "all the cunning of her diplomatic race" and as possessing the "dark eyes . . . [of] an Italian assassin." The opportunities for anarchy offered by the American frontier compound Cage's innate southern European love of treachery by bringing out in him, as once they had in Lawson's lost Englishmen, "the savage, which is restrained in human beings only by the artificial checks of civilization." But Shackelford, who is just as strongly opposed to Queen Elizabeth and the monarchical system she represents as ever Bancroft was, entertains more than a passing doubt about the socially disruptive tendencies of democracy as well. In her version of the story it is a low-life upstart named (by a strange literary coincidence) Jake Barnes who, after conniving to get himself elected governor of the Lost Colony by the votes of the ignorant rabble, commits the murder of an Indian, which brings down the wrath of the red men on the colony's head.

This engraving was used as an illustration in E. A. B. Shackelford's book *Virginia Dare: A Romance of the Sixteenth Century* (New York: Thomas Whittaker, 1892). Shackelford's was the first of the Roanoke tales to challenge George Bancroft's Jacksonian democratic interpretation of the story.

In Shackelford's view, the infant Virginia Dare is on the one hand a symbol of the natural aristocracy and, on the other, so perfect a paradigm of the Christian virtue of humility that she is mistaken for a goddess by Pocahontas when the two accidentally meet. Virginia's career epitomizes the political moral of knowing and maintaining one's own place in the grand scheme of things and of unquestioningly accepting the lot that God has given. "Who can tell what a pure brave life will do?" Shackelford asks sententiously. "Lived in a humble station in this nineteenth Century, or in the wild forest three hundred years ago, as was VIRGINIA DARE's!"

From Shackleford, the saga passed to another author who shared some of her political views but had a different notion about what fate had befallen Virginia Dare. Like Mrs. M. M., Sallie Southall Cotten claimed that her story, *The White Doe: The Fate of Virginia Dare, An Indian Legend* (1901), was based on Indian lore. Also like Mrs. M. M., Mrs. Cotten, a dedicated daughter of the American Revolution once famed as a feminist (the Julia Ward Howe of the South, as she was called) and founder of the short-lived Virginia Dare Columbian Memorial Association, had rather obviously learned her Indian material from some questionable Indians—Ovid and the anonymous authors of the Irish folksong "Molly Bawn" among them—but no one seems to have been particularly bothered by that problem at the time. Not one to put down Pocahontas, whom she honored, Mrs. Cotten nevertheless demanded equal rights for another woman who, along with the fabled Indian princess, deserved a place of honor in the pan-

Sallie Southall Cotten (1846-1929), like Mrs. M. M., claimed that her story *The White Doe: The Fate of Virginia Dare, An Indian Legend* (Philadelphia: J. B. Lippincott, 1901) was based on Indian lore. In Mrs. Cotten's tale Virginia Dare is adopted by Manteo's tribe after the fall of Roanoke, renamed Winona, and transformed by an evil magician into a white doe. Engraving from Samuel A. Ashe and others (eds.), *Biographical History of North Carolina from Colonial Times to the Present* (Greensboro: Charles L. Van Noppen, 8 volumes, 1905-1917), VII, facing p. 122.

theon of American women heroes. To prove her point, she produced a poem in romping Hiawathans, framed by a prologue in meter reminiscent of *Sir Gawain and the Green Knight* and an epilogue in elongated Hiawathans.

In *The White Doe,* Virginia, adopted by Manteo's tribe after the fall of Roanoke and renamed Winona (the "Snow Papoose"), gets transformed into a white doe by an evil magician who has vowed that if he cannot have her, neither can her chosen Indian lover, O-kis-ko. But the resourceful O-kis-ko procures a magic arrow to change Winona back into a maiden again, only to have another evil Indian, our old friend Wanchese, join in the tribal hunt for the strange white deer who is driving all the other animals from the local hunting ground and release his arrow at the same moment as O-kis-ko. Normally, that would not have mattered much, since the doe is, like the one in Mrs. M. M.'s story, unaffected by ordinary weapons; but Wanchese's arrow has been tipped with an arrowhead made from a silver brooch given to him by an English lady when he visited England, and it drives home to its mark right beside O-kis-ko's magic shaft. O-kis-ko strives desperately to revive his beloved with waters from a magic spring, but this dries up when "Blood of Pale-Face shed by Red Man" is mixed with its waters. As the waters recede, however,

This representation of the "beautiful white maiden" Winona, painted by May Louise Barrett in 1901, was used as the frontispiece of Sallie Southall Cotten's *The White Doe.*

there appears a tiny shoot of the scuppernong grape, which previously had grown only as a white variety but now produces red grapes as well. Before we condemn Mrs. Cotten's work as merely a prophetic endorsement of a popular wine, we would do well to examine her explanation for all this fantasy:

> For we know the silver arrow, fatal to all
> sorcery
> Was the gleaming light of Progress, speeding
> from across the sea,
> Before which the Red Man vanished, shrinking
> from its silvery light
> As the magic waters yielded to the silver
> arrow's blight.
> And the tiny shoot with leaflets, by the
> sunlight warmed to life,
> Was the Vine of Civilization in the wilderness
> of strife. . . .

Despite the unintentional ambiguity of her language—she does, after all, call the symbol of civilization a "blight"—Mrs. Cotten here shows herself a confirmed convert to the gospel of American progress. Nearly as interesting as her allegory, then, is her prefatory excursion into historical typology, a brand of interpretation that would have done credit to George Bancroft or, for that matter, Cotton Mather. The reflection that Admiral Dewey's flagship at Manila Bay was named the *Raleigh,* for example, inspires an encomium to that hero's pioneering spirit and a meditation on the "Nemesis of fate" that had pursued the Spaniards and, three hundred years after they had intrigued against the happiness of Roanoke, brought about their defeat at the hands of a nation spiritually descended from the noble Sir Walter.

The historical pattern of "universal progress" stands revealed to Mrs. Cotten from the perspective of America's emergence as an international military power at the end of the nineteenth century, and her vision enables her to pronounce that historical events "must be estimated . . . with reference to their ultimate results" and interpreted according to the "ideals of the people" who had lived through them or look back upon them. Thus, the fall of Roanoke, contrary to what John Lawson had claimed almost two centuries earlier, did not represent the end of something but instead predicted the long-deferred victory of civilization over savagery on the one hand and over the forces of idolatry, tyranny, and greedy imperialism on the other. It was a triumph for the English heritage of laws and customs, a Protestant ideal achieved by the sons and daughters of those born during the flowering of English culture. George Bancroft might have said it more cautiously, but he could not have said it more unequivocally. Among the most tentative of the Roanoke romances in its handling of the intertwined issues of race and sex, Mrs. Cotten's *The White Doe* is nonetheless perhaps the most straightforwardly optimistic of all the stories involving the Lost Colony and Virginia Dare and makes a fitting conclusion to the nineteenth-century phase of the romance.

IV. Passion, Primitivism, Prevarication, and Parody: Twentieth-Century Discourses and Disclosures

And so, weary and footsore, the straggling remnants of Roanoke struggle onward, arriving with the rest of us in the bewildering world of the twentieth century. In 1901 William Farquhar Payson's *John Vytal: A Tale of the Lost Colony* found them once more swamped by Indians and Spaniards and scurrying for cover at Croatoan in a conclusion that Payson rather too hopefully suggested would be something we had not heard before. But he was right in one respect: no one had previously thought of bringing Christopher Marlowe to America for even a brief visit or had yet connected his death in a tavern brawl with a mission that, had he not been so hot-headed, might have saved the settlement. As things worked out, he failed to reach the queen with news of an impending Spanish invasion of the colony; and so Ralegh's dream of an English empire in America, the airy vision of an age still able to imagine great events, fell victim to Renaissance rashness.

Less successful at finding something new to say about Virginia Dare and Roanoke was W. H. Moore, author of a long poem entitled "Virginia Dare: A Story of Colonial Days" (1904). Moore had pretty clearly heard about Sallie Southall Cotten's white doe of Virginia, and he may have glanced into E. A. B. Shackelford's tale as well before starting his own story, intended at least in part as a paean to "Liberty! Liberty!" for whose "dear sake,/What costly sacrifices men do make." Moore rechristens Ananias Dare with the "more poetical and euphonious" name of David, turns Eleanor into Jennie ("the diminutive of Virginia"), and invents an Indian named Laska, son of Manteo, to serve as Virginia's suitor and eventual husband. Thus is ensured the appearance in America of "a hardier stock" than English blood alone could have produced, a race of heroes who "o'er this Western world should wield their rod." Arguably the worst poet in the history of the world, Moore limps along through seventy-three interminable stanzas innocent alike of metrical interest, memorable metaphors or images (except those memorable for their absurdity, that is), and all poetical merit. His conclusion that Virginia's life

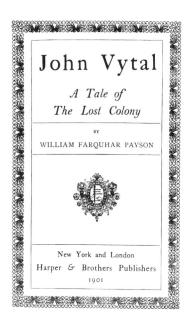

John Vytal

A Tale of
The Lost Colony

BY

WILLIAM FARQUHAR PAYSON

New York and London
Harper & Brothers Publishers
1901

In William Farquhar Payson's *John Vytal: A Tale of the Lost Colony* (1901) the fate of the Roanoke colonists is sealed by the failure of Christopher Marlowe, having journeyed to America, to reach Queen Elizabeth with news of an impending Spanish invasion of the colony. The title page of Payson's work is shown at left.

"though lost, is found in endless worth" offers a pretty fair sample of the talent and insight he brings to his task and leaves us exactly where most other Roanoke writers have left us: with a last-ditch assertion that Virginia and her lost associates somehow mattered very much in the history of humanity but with the same old vagueness about just what their importance might have been.

Moore's handling of the marital material of the Roanoke legend tends to confirm a drift within the saga in the direction of a marginal primitivism sanctified, however, only by the promise of American progress in centuries still to unfold. His dilemma and his solution, at any rate, are by now familiar ones in the Roanoke story. If America is in any way to be imagined as arising from the fruitful loins of Virginia Dare, as by this time in the telling seems an essential part of the story, then Virginia must perforce be provided with a husband. Cornelia Tuthill's inspired invention of the dazed Jamestown wanderer Henry Johnson notwithstanding, only Indians seem to be truly available to take on the job. But this unpalatable fact—for the romance has not yet arrived at the unabashed celebration of passion and primitivism that will mark it in the twentieth century—can at least be ameliorated if not entirely denied by providing a fictional rather than a real historical Indian as a husband and by making sure, as Moore does, that the husband learns to read and write and to adopt his wife's religion. In this, Moore has taken only one step further than Sallie Southall Cotten and E. A. B. Shackelford.

Thanks largely to the 1907 tercentenary of the founding of Jamestown, Moore did not have the last word about the Lost Colonists for very long. Two novels extending and enlarging upon the matter of Roanoke appeared in 1908: William Thomas Wilson's *For the Love of Lady Margaret* and Mary Virginia Wall's *The Daughter of Virginia Dare.* Wilson's novel is only peripherally concerned with the lore of the Lost Colony; its hero, Sir Thomas Winchester, actually proves ungallant enough to rescue his beloved, Lady Margaret Carroll, from improbable captivity in America but leaves the Lost Colonists to find themselves if they can. Mary Virginia Wall's novel, on the other hand, despite regaling us with an all-too-predictable story of massacre and adoption of the infant Virginia by the friendly Croatan Indians, makes a significant contribution to the saga by arranging for Powhatan to kidnap Virginia and force her to become his wife. Virginia's daughter, then, turns out to be none other than the fabled Pocahontas, the logical issue of a genealogy that American writers had been trying for years to establish. If the luckless explorers of Jamestown had but possessed sense enough to know that Pocahon-

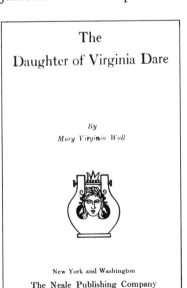

The
Daughter of Virginia Dare

By
Mary Virginia Wall

New York and Washington
The Neale Publishing Company
1908

In Mary Virginia Wall's *The Daughter of Virginia Dare* (1908) Virginia Dare is kidnapped by the Indian chief Powhatan and forced to become his wife. Virginia later gives birth to a daughter, who turns out to be the fabled Indian princess Pocahontas.

tas's kindness toward them could have arisen only from the white blood in her veins, they would have understood that the secret of Ralegh's missing settlers lay in front of their noses all the while.

Ushered at last into the mysteries of her own sexuality, even if the crucial deed of darkness had to be performed by a savage whose embrace she detested, Virginia Dare becomes predictably more prolific, and in some cases dangerously so. There is no special problem of this sort with Paul Green's symphonic drama *The Lost Colony* (1937), performed annually on Roanoke Island in ritualistic celebration of Virginia's birthday and the fate of the outcasts, or with the pageant that preceded Green's, Frederick Henry Koch's *Raleigh, the Shepherd of the Ocean* (1920), a play with an announced "two-fold purpose,— praise to Walter Raleigh, / And with fair England,—union, brotherhood." Written at the height of nationalistic euphoria over the outcome of the First World War, Koch's paean to the spirit of American youth in consort joined with British wisdom and valor to defeat German tyranny was a period piece even as it issued from the press, and it pales beside Mary Johnston's reluctant acknowledgment of Virginia Dare's alienation from the march of history in *Croatan* (1923) and Herbert Bouldin Hawes's *The Daughter of the Blood* (1930).

In many ways the most interesting of all the Roanoke novels, though not the best, Hawes's book changes Virginia into an apparent Indian maiden named Nonya, unabashed priestess of the post-Freudian cult of primitivism. Through much of the novel, Nonya-Virginia races around the forest fainting at appropriate intervals, giving orders to the awe-stricken Indians who regard her as a goddess, talking the language of deer and even rattlesnakes, and finally attempting to arrange a wedding between the libidinous Captain John Smith—who at one point tries to seduce her—and the Princess Pocahontas. This attempt to smooth out the rough edges of a romance with which the Lost Colony has become progressively associated fails, of course, but in a provocative preface Hawes explains his reasons for giving it a try. Virginia Dare, he confesses, had long been the idol of his boyhood fantasies, but only after a long winter of artistic impotency did she condescend to appear to him in the guise of his personal muse, silently commanding him to forget about all the earlier fantasies and write instead about her symbolic role as the mythic mother of America. It is a large order for anyone to have filled, and if Hawes does not

Raleigh

THE SHEPHERD OF THE OCEAN

A Pageant-Drama

BY

FREDERICK HENRY KOCH

Professor of Dramatic Literature in the University of North Carolina

DESIGNED TO COMMEMORATE THE TERCENTENARY OF
THE EXECUTION OF SIR WALTER RALEIGH

With a Foreword by
Edwin Greenlaw

PRINTED AT
Raleigh, North Carolina
BY EDWARDS & BROUGHTON PRINTING CO.
MCMXX

The Roanoke Colony Memorial Association
of Manteo, North Carolina

With the Cooperation of

THE NORTH CAROLINA HISTORICAL COMMISSION, THE
ROANOKE ISLAND HISTORICAL ASSOCIATION, INC.;
and THE FEDERAL THEATRE PROJECT AND
OTHER AGENCIES OF THE WORKS
PROGRESS ADMINISTRATION

presents

The Lost Colony

(An outdoor play with music, dance and pantomime)

by

PAUL GREEN

Staged and Directed

by

SAMUEL SELDEN

Supervising Director.............FREDERICK H. KOCH, *Director*
The Carolina Playmakers

Musical Director............ERLE STAPLETON, *State Director*
Federal Music Project

Production Associate.....MRS. ALEXANDER MATHIS, *Director*
The Elizabethan Players of Manteo

Roanoke Island Waterside Theatre
ROANOKE ISLAND, NORTH CAROLINA
July 4, 1937 to September 6, 1937

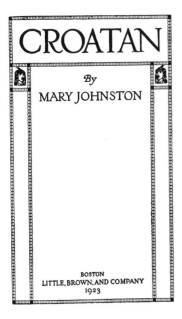

Frederick Henry Koch's "pageant-drama" *Raleigh, the Shepherd of the Ocean* was written in 1920 "to commemorate the tercentenary of the execution of Sir Walter Raleigh." Paul Green's play *The Lost Colony*, written and first performed in 1937, is North Carolina's oldest outdoor drama, having been presented each summer since that time (except during World War II) at the Waterside Theater in Manteo. Mary Johnston's *Croatan* was published in 1923. The title page of each of these works is shown here.

In Herbert Bouldin Hawes's *The Daughter of the Blood* (Boston: Four Seas Company, c. 1930) Virginia appears as an apparent Indian maiden named Nonya. This and two similar photographs of an unidentified woman dressed in deerskins were used as illustrations in Hawes's book.

entirely succeed, the fault is probably Virginia's as much as it is his own comparative lack of talent.

Hawes's *Daughter of the Blood* was followed by Clifford Wayne Hartridge's *Manteo* (1935), by all odds the best of the Roanoke novels. The book tells the story of a half-breed descendant of the first governor of Roanoke (this would have been Ralph Lane, though it isn't in

Manteo (1935), a novel by Clifford Wayne Hartridge, tells the story of a half-breed descendant of the first governor of Roanoke and an Indian princess. The novel's title page is shown at right.

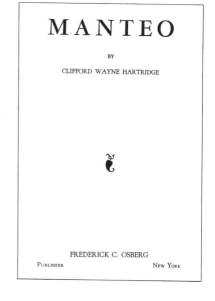

MANTEO

BY

CLIFFORD WAYNE HARTRIDGE

FREDERICK C. OSBERG
PUBLISHER   NEW YORK

the novel) and an Indian princess. Born and reared in English society, Manteo finds himself as much an outcast as Pocahontas must have been during her brief life in England. Manteo eventually joins General Oglethorpe's expedition to America, becomes a masterful frontiersman, earns the identity denied him in civilized London, and discovers true love with a wild Indian maiden named Manteona, the great granddaughter of Manteo and a half-breed like the hero himself. Structured around the image of the circle, symbol at one and the same time of unity and wholeness as well as of the emptiness, the vacuum, that the Lost Colony signifies, Hartridge's novel also points to interesting parallels between legendary lapses in English history and the mystery of the Lost Colony as a way of enlarging his hero's quest for personal identity into a broader cultural enterprise.

What happened next in the sage of the Lost Colonists can only be regarded as an astonishing illustration of the old saw that truth is indeed sometimes stranger than fiction. In the spring of 1939 the historian Haywood J. Pearce, Jr., announced to an astounded if tiny readership of the Brenau College *Bulletin* that a recently discovered twenty-one-pound quartz stone promised to unlock once and for all the riddle of Roanoke. In seventeen engraved lines over the initials "EWD" (presumably Eleanor White Dare), the stone sketched a story of "misarie & Warre," forced removal, murder, and treachery of the darkest dye.

The alleged discovery of this 21-pound quartz stone in a swamp near Edenton, North Carolina, in 1937 precipitated the celebrated Dare Stone Hoax. Photograph from Boyden Sparkes, "Writ on Rocke," *Saturday Evening Post*, 213 (April 26, 1941), p. 10.

Following the publication of Pearce's speculations in the prestigious *Journal of Southern History,* the renowned and hitherto remote Harvard historian Samuel Eliot Morison was called into the case and, somewhat incredibly, pronounced the stone a genuine relic of the Elizabethan age. Soon more stones were discovered near the town of Pelzer, South Carolina, and along the Chattahoochee River in Hall County, Georgia, each one adding precious details to the story: "Father we goe sw" and "Father the salvage shew moche mercye . . . ," the stones declared. The general migration of the colonists appeared to be in the direction of what yet another stone identified as the "primeval splendor" of Florida. By now even Cecil B. DeMille had got wind of the strange goings-on in Georgia and the Carolinas and was said to be considering an epic movie about the mystery of Roanoke. In all, some twenty-seven stones turned up, each one duly surrendered for the inspection and, generally, the approval of eager historians.

Samuel Eliot Morison (*left*), then a professor of history at Harvard University, examined the so-called Dare Stone and pronounced it a genuine relic of the Elizabethan age. Shown with Morison is Haywood J. Pearce, Jr., then professor of history at Emory University, Atlanta, and vice-president of Brenau College, Gainesville, Georgia. Photograph by Pete Roton; from Sparkes, "Writ on Rocke," p. 10.

But then the bubble burst. Intrigued by the tale as recounted by Professor Pearce, the *Saturday Evening Post* sent a reporter by the name of Boyden Sparkes to learn what he could about the story, and what he learned was that professors of history sometimes neglect to ask the kinds of questions that come as second nature to trained journalists. Sparkes's inquiries soon revealed a morass of contradictions and strange coincidences that eventually pointed the finger of fraud inescapably in the direction of the stonemason *cum* moonshiner who had made and reported the find in the first place. Nevertheless, so dissatisfied do Americans seem to be with this one lapse in an otherwise continuous historical narrative that as late as 1964 an angry reporter for a Georgia newspaper, ignoring entirely the evidence presented in Sparkes's 1941 exposure, railed at the stupidity of blockhead historians who refused to look again into the valuable clues about the Lost Colony then gathering dust in the locked basements of Brenau.

If it accomplished nothing else, the Dare Stone Hoax, as it soon came to be called, at least inspired the first and only lighthearted literary treatment of the Roanoke story. This was Mrs. Mayhew Paul's "Lay of the Lost Colony," published by Nell Battle Lewis in her column in the *Uplift* on August 16, 1941 (as close to Virginia Dare's anniversary as the publication schedule would allow, one supposes). The poem, Lewis claims, "throws bright new light on those mysterious original immigrants and . . . incidentally backs as archaeological evidence fully equal, if not superior, to that furnished by the Brenau stones." The verses constitute so delightful a spoof of the hubbub over the Dare Stones that they deserve quotation at some length:

> Dame Eleanor Dare, by her log-cabin door,
> With mallet and chisel and tomb-stones galore,
> Sat busily knocking out tender adieux
> In dozens of delicate stone billets-doux.
> Virginia Dare squalled and the pot bubbled o'er,
> But Eleanor only did hammer the more!
> With rare intuition, to which she paid heed,
> She felt that some day she would probably need
> A few such mementoes to sprinkle her trail
> To tell future searchers the pitiful tale;
> And knowing with Indians behind every pine,
> She'd never have time to drop papa a line.
> So like the wise babes in the wood she did plan
> To carve a few letters to strew as she ran.

When the Indians do at last attack, the colonists are so burdened by Eleanor's tablets that they are easily captured by the red men, who, regarding the rocks as "great totems rare" because the English have taken so much trouble to preserve them, make the captive colonists continue to carry the stones. Then the narrative resumes:

The trail it was long and the way it was hard,
And brambles and briars their steps did retard,
But onward they plodded, though bloody the track,
Each bearing a page of El's book on his back.
And as one by one in exhaustion they fell,
With stones at their side the sad story to tell,
The band was depleted until there were none
Left living at all when the journey was done!
The centuries passed and no one ever found
These marvelous relics till men, scratching round,
By greatest good fortune, the very same year
The pageant at Manteo was to appear,
Discovered the things to our bug-eyed surprise—
Which happening naturally helped advertise.
Now Heaven forbid I give any offense,
But wasn't that wonderful coincidence?

Apparently as impervious to parody as they had already proved
to be to Spanish armaments and Indian arrows, the Lost Colonists
continued their quest for a place—any place—to call home. But her
mother's masonic indiscretions may have doomed Virginia Dare.
After Hawes's *Daughter of the Blood,* the Dare Stone Hoax, and Paul's
poem, at any rate, Virginia all but disappears from Roanoke romances,
or, if she is allowed to exist at all, she remains an infant and perforce
a peripheral figure. In 1942, for example, H. K. Russell contributed
to the pages of *Poet Lore* and to the romance of Roanoke an ambitious
and accomplished poem entitled "Mark Bennett on Roanoke." Bennett, the poet-hero of Russell's piece, is left at the end with his Indian bride Amosens to rear the infant Virginia after all the other
settlers and, for good measure, the Croatan Indians as well have been
massacred by Wanchese's followers. Virginia's birth inspires a
separate section of the poem, as was perhaps inevitable, given the
material with which Russell was working, and Bennett himself appears "like the shepherd/ In the pageant" to present his gift to the
infant of the Outer Banks. But this babe, however blessed she may
appear to be, poses no effective counterforce to the chaos and violence
chronicled in a narrative darkly shadowed by the fable of the Fall
and organized around episodes with titles like "Blood-Doom" and
"The Sword." Some of the unfortunate colonists, it is true, may have
come, as Mark Bennett claims, "To find what we had never had/ But
felt we'd lost," but the point of view that prevails in the poem may
be found in other lines, Dick Shabedge's scornful and cynical admis-

sion that " 'There's that/ Inside me writhes at Eden innocence.' "

"Mark Bennett on Roanoke" is steeped in neurotic sexuality. Women throughout are presented mainly as old hags or indifferently promiscuous wives and widows, and the men who find them so loathsome—this is true even of Mark Bennett for a while—work off their wrath against them by destroying the Indians and the land. In turn, death in America claims its victims through sadistic and perversely sexual weapons—'the bone-tipped wood . . . is poisoned/ To burn up the blood'—and comes in the guise of sexual consummation:

> Time,
> For the splitting of a moment, hangs on the upswing,
> Then plunges at the downward arc to measure out
> This fraction of eternity.

The preoccupation with sex and violence and death that informs "Mark Bennett on Roanoke," dark and disturbing though it may seem in a romance that had begun pretty much in Arcadian innocence, merely provides a prelude to some of the novels that came after Russell's poem. Retaining at least vestigal reverance for Virginia Dare's historical purity, for example, Don Tracy can work Virginia into *Roanoke Renegade* (1954) only by following Russell's lead and keeping her a child, blissfully uncontaminated by the sexual license with which the American wilderness then seems to have become identified. Tracy's hero, Dionysius Harvie (an intentional corruption of Dionys Harvie, one of the original settlers), conquers Indian wenches, London prostitutes, and the American continent with an orgiastic energy that leaves the reader—but never our stalwart hero—wrenched and sweaty and gasping for breath. A hairsbreadth this side of pornography, Tracy's novel nevertheless manages to come through with an important statement about the fire in the blood and the mercantile rapacity, easily translated into the symbolism of insatiate sexuality, that contribute dark background tones to the portraits in the gallery of merchant-pirates like Drake and Hawkins and even Ralegh himself, whom Americans have otherwise so much admired.

Closely akin to Tracy's brand of erotic adventurism is Edison Marshall's *The Lost Colony* (1964), a rather hefty volume that, not satisfied with the mystery as it stands, also offers its readers "instructions in anthropology, natural history, mythology, geography, and psychology."

A fair sample of Marshall's anthropological lore might be the curious custom of depilation among the Croatan Indians, or perhaps the appearance of a Sioux woman in South Carolina who offers herself to our hero, Martyn Sutton, and, no novice in such matters, claims to know "all the little tricks of muscle that men love."

In Marshall's version of the story, a tale of nearly endless flight and pursuit that eventually induces hallucinations of timelessness and deja vu in the fugitives (and the reader), the survivors of the Lost Colony finally establish a refuge among a lost tribe of Florida Indians and dispatch Sutton back to Roanoke to await their English deliverers. He arrives on the same evening that Governor White's expedition returns, reflectively gazes seaward for a while and thinks about his old life in England, then deliberately carves the word "CROATOAN" in a tree to leave a false trail and turns his back forever upon civilization. His rejection rounds out a psychological adventure novel that has been explicitly based on the premise that "the forces bringing about the evacuation of Roanoke Island were already at work among certain members of the colony before they left England."

Apart from a few hundred historical improbabilities of this sort, what especially distinguishes Marshall's novel is that it is a veritable Freudian's delight, a work that begins with a son's being suspected of having murdered his mother, includes the ritualistic sacrifice of a daughter by her father, and ends with the slaying of a pale druidic priestess("the arrow . . . struck Winifred in her soft and beautiful throat that I had kissed, then plunged deep") who throughout has made the hero's life alternately exciting and miserable and has jealously attempted to stand in the way of his affair with a rescued Indian lass, Weechee. The opening scenes of the story are played out in the shadow of Stonehenge, symbol of England's own lost and silent ancestry, and there is even a fanatical Puritan preacher among the surviving colonists who speaks a language all too familiar in Roanoke romances when he denounces intermarriage as "the sin for which God punished His children." In this scriptural context, we can see Martyn as a mad and murderous Moses attempting to lead his people out of the wilderness and into the promised land; but paradise never materializes, and one of the central questions about the Lost Colony that the novel raises is phrased not in biblical but in classical terms: "Had someone in our party aroused the furies from their foul nests? Must we expiate ancient evil in battle and bloodshed?"

As for Virginia Dare, she is scarcely in evidence at all; but her lurking presence is, however, felt throughout in the strong antifeminism that dominates the novel and in the contrasting characters of the pale Winifred, the priestess who initiates the hero into life's sexual mysteries but whose possession of occult and darkly secret knowledge links her with Virginia and threatens the hero's sovereignty and freedom, and the Indian maiden Weechee, from whose promise of uninhibited sexual experience the hero also mysteriously turns. Weechee's death and the hero's rejection of Elizabeth's England, with all that this gesture implies about Martyn's refusal to accept the complexities of history and guilt, dramatize a striking regression toward infantile irresponsibility and gratification, which, in the broadest sense, may be said to constitute the plot of the novel.

Like most descents into decadence, the transformation of the Roanoke story into erotic spectacle, signaling as it seems to a modern suspicion that the materials alone can no longer hold reader interest, may be taken as a sign that the romance is at last on the verge of exhaustion. Absent the eroticism of Bennett's poem and Tracy's and Marshall's novels, at any rate, the story seems to have survived since the 1940s largely on the strength of its appeal to juvenile audiences. This is the case, for example, with both Jim Kjelgaard's "Croatan" in *Buckskin Brigade* (1947), which once again presents Simon Fernandes in the role of traitor, and Jean Bothwell's *Lost Colony* (1953), which likewise blames Spanish treachery for the disappearance of the settlement. Beyond such works for adolescent readers, the final two fictional interpretations of the Roanoke material to date, Jesse

This drawing by Edward F. Cortese is reproduced in Jean Bothwell's *Lost Colony: The Mystery of Roanoke Island* (New York: Holt, Rinehart and Winston, 1953). Bothwell's book, like many others, attributes the disappearance of the Lost Colony to Spanish treachery.

Stuart's *Daughter of the Legend* and Philip José Farmer's *Dare* (both 1965), use history only as a point of embarkation for far more modern fables; both works, moreover, are twenty years old as of this writing, a longer lapse than any other since Cornelia L. Tuthill first reclaimed the story in 1840. Again, this seems to suggest that the story has played itself out, but no one should be surprised to see it reappear in defiance of all predictive evidence to the contrary. Of such miraculous recoveries, after all, has the fabric of the legend been woven from the start.

It may be, in fact, that Jesse Stuart's *Daughter of the Legend* points the way, although imperfectly, toward a recovery of relevance for the Roanoke adventurers. Stuart's book, as has been said, makes use of the Lost Colony only peripherally as one of several possible explanations for the origins of the Melungeons, a strange breed of mountain people whose genesis remains unexplained to this day. " 'You remember Sir Walter Raleigh's Lost Colony?' " one of the characters asks Dave Stoneking, the hero. " 'There was never a trace of it found. It's believed they were captured by the Cherokee Indians and brought to this mountain and here they mixed with the Indians.' " One of the Melungeons himself, Don Praytor, makes clear the psychological implications of such uncertain ancestry when he declares, " 'We're Melungeons! . . . We're hated! Despised. We're a lost people.' " But Stuart, writing out of the heightened racial consciousness of the mid-sixties, is less interested in psychology than in social injustice. His tale concerns the ostracism of Stoneking for having the audacity to marry a Melungeon, Deutsia Huntoon, and mixing his white blood with hers. With her death in childbirth and Stoneking's defeat by the forces of intolerance, the book reaches a bleak conclusion—though while Deutsia lives, it seems that love will conquer all. Deutsia also gives every indication of being the true heir of the wild huntress Virginia Dare when at a revival meeting she strokes a large rattlesnake. Thesis-ridden and overly sentimental at many moments, Stuart's novel may well be the worst book he has ever written; but it deserves attention here as the first of the Roanoke stories since George Parson Lathrop's *True* to confront openly the racial issues that Sir Richard Grenville's haughty treatment of the Indians had made an inseparable part of the tale two hundred years and more before the saga of Roanoke ever got under way in earnest.*

The same racial issues concern Philip José Farmer in his science-fiction extravaganza *Dare,* named for a planet named for (of course) Ananias Dare. On this planet, where iron is scarce and weaponry therefore remains primitive, the remote descendants of the Lost Colonists live in uneasy coexistence with the "horstels," a strange race of creatures with entirely human features except for their long horse-like tails (thus the name "horstels," which is also a play on "hostiles") and the long fur on their legs. This detail, incidentally, Farmer may have picked up from Russell's "Mark Bennett on Roanoke." Against all his racial prejudices, the hero, Jack Cage (the name of the villain in Edward Ingle's "Roanoke"), falls in love with R'li, a princess of the horstels; but their love affair is chronicled against the growing tension between horstels and humans, whose HK (horstel killer) society clearly represents an interplanetary version of the Ku Klux Klan. Eventually the murder of an innocent horstel and a staged attack on government troops by men dressed as horstels (a parodic version, apparently, of the Boston Tea Party) provokes open warfare and the imminent destruction of the horstels, who are portrayed throughout as peace-loving and gentle children of nature. At this dramatic moment, in a nice but, alas, only wishful reversal of history, white men arrive from the planet earth and impose and enforce a permanent peace between the two races. "We will hate no one and hope that no one hates us," says R'li on the final page of the book, "knowing full well that there is as much hate as love in this world." With this restatement of the original dreams of Roanoke in uneasy juxtaposition to historical reality, the final contribution as of this writing to the romance of Roanoke comes to its poignant conclusion.

---

*This seems the proper place to acknowledge William S. Powell's fine study, *Paradise Preserved: A History of the Roanoke Island Historical Association* (Chapel Hill: University of North Carolina Press, 1965), which includes a bibliography of Roanoke literature. I have not been able to read every work Powell lists there, but I have been able to add several with which he was unfamiliar. Additionally, it should be noted that Inglis Fletcher's *Roanoke Hundred,* which may be the most popular of all stories about the Roanoke settlement, has not been treated here because it is not about the Lost Colony but rather about Ralegh's first settlement.

V. Some Speculations at the End: The Lost Colony as American Myth and Symbol

In some ways, it is not difficult to understand why Americans have been so strongly attached to the story of the Lost Colony and the adventures of Virginia Dare. As one of the most flexible of American historical metaphors, the tale lends itself equally well to praise of progress or of primitivism, staid middle-class stability or almost unrestrained eroticism. The saga also features a peripheral cast of characters who, as the historian Graham Daves calls their roll, have long fascinated the popular American imagination, obsessed as it seems to be with the great Elizabethan age of swash and buckle: "Elizabeth, the Virgin Queen; Raleigh, the *preux chevalier,* soldier, statesman, poet, historian; Sir Richard Grenville, sailor, soldier and martyr; Sir Francis Drake, Admiral and circumnavigator of the globe." Oddly missing from this list are two other slightly later names, John Smith and Pocahontas, who in themselves might have been sufficient to ensure a continuing American interest in the tale, if only as an adjunct to another of America's favorite stories. There is also the nearly universal appeal of a good mystery, the chance to match wits against perhaps the most reticent sphinx in the American past, so that, all in all, it is hardly surprising to find that the Lost Colonists have survived in our imaginations so many years after their very dust has vanished from the earth.

Related to this appeal is the simple but perhaps still more powerful attraction of Arcadian innocence, the dream of escape from modernism through retreat into a green and golden past. This pastoral, even Edenic, element has been a part of the meaning of Roanoke ever since Captain Arthur Barlowe's initial voyage of exploration inspired his report of "shole water, which smelt so sweeetly . . . as if we had bene in the midst of some delicate garden, abounding with all kinds of odoriferous flowers. . . . I thinke in all the world the like abundance is not to be founde. . . ."

For the authors of the romances, indeed, the appeal of the escape must be even stronger than it is to the imagination of the rest of us, for the story offers—or seems to offer—release from the authority of history as well. The problem is, of course, that it is only the primeval silence that is so alluring: once words begin to fill the void of history, all vestiges of absolute authorial freedom vanish and the conventions of literature and myth take over the tale, dictating within broad but nevertheless clearly delimited (and delimiting) imaginative bounds all events to be narrated. Further, the sound of the narrative voice itself is alone sufficient to dispel the Arcadian dream, breaking the silence that is the real reason for our interest in the romance and filling it with conjectures that cannot hold our interest, however elaborate and exciting they may be, nearly so much as that single enigmatic word, "CROATOAN."

Yet, Arcadian romance is one thing and history—or so we like to think—quite another. We can understand some of the appeal of Roanoke for fantasizers and fiction makers, but why should sane and sober historians still seek for clues among the ancient rubble? Some reasons seem entirely legitimate. According to Richard Slotkin's *Regeneration through Violence* (1973), for instance, one of the "peculiar forces that shaped American mythology" and, in turn, the American's sense of his or her own destiny and history was what Slotkin calls "the sense of exile—the psychological anxieties in tearing up the home roots for wide wandering outward in space and, apparently, backward in time." This sense of loss, Slotkin goes on to say, "was heightened by the inevitable lapsing of communication with the homeland, the divergence of colonial from homeland historical experience, and the rise of new generations more accultured or acclimated to the wilderness, less like the remembered grandparents in the fixed image of Europe." Although Slotkin does not mention Sir Walter Ralegh or the Roanoke settlements in his study, it is doubtful whether the history of English colonization in North America can offer a more startling example, a purer metaphor, of the complex sense of loss experienced by those who abandoned the mother country for the New World than can the story of the Lost Colony and its most famous citizen, Virginia Dare. The Lost Colonists have, literally, dropped out of time and very nearly out of historical consciousness altogether, and only the determination of American historians that we shall not lose touch forever and absolutely with this clue to *our* cultural heritage—that we shall not ourselves suffer the extreme dislocation of the colonists, that is—preserves them in our memory.

It may be, indeed, that historians find themselves compelled by the fate of the Lost Colony for yet another reason, one intimately tied to the nature of history itself: is the past, however deep the documentation, at all recoverable? Or are there, as many modern historians appear to believe, only different degrees of ignorance about the lives that went before our own? If this latter be true, small wonder that the disappearance of Ralegh's colonists, who left but one text, one clue to their whereabouts and fate carved on a tree, continues to fascinate the historical mind out of all proportion to any facts that we might still hope to learn about them. That single clue "CROATOAN," a word wonderfully derived from the language of the new and unknown world rather than from the languages of Europe, stands like a secret, talismanic utterance at the very threshold of our history and as a symbol in the extreme of the whole historical enterprise itself.

Yet, in themselves, the reasons just provided seem inadequate to account for the persistence of the story in our culture or for the energy that has been invested in retelling it over the years. What is there about the tale, we might legitimately ask, that in both art's and erring reason's spite convinces us that it is important enough to bear retelling, not once but literally dozens of times? Why do we keep coming back to it?

One plausible answer to those questions comes from, of all unlikely places, a letter written pseudonymously to the well-known advice-to-the-love-and-otherwise-lorn columnist Ann Landers, one of whose correspondents wrote to record for posterity the psychological trauma endured by an orphaned or adopted child when he comes to contemplate the question of his own true origins. "There's this big break in my life," the writer begins. "I need to find my real parents. . . . My imagination runs wild when I think about what might have happened that made them abandon me." Though Landers replied only that "you seem obsessed," the remarks offered by three psychologists—Anna Freud, Joseph Goldstein, and Albert J. Solnit— seem more to the point: "Adolescents frequently institute a search for the lost and unknown parents, as a step preliminary to achieving independence from any parental authority and reaching maturity." While this may sound like no more than an accidentally accurate description of what goes on in the Roanoke romances, it is probably worth noting that the story first broke into American literature at roughly the adolescent stage in our national development and that, as we have noticed before, the search for the true parents is a major theme in Revolutionary rhetoric.

America, it seems fair to say, is a country that came into its independence, but scarcely into its mature identity, by the deliberate act of declaring itself a waif among nations, creating afterward a version of the old family image under Federalist and neo-Federalist policies. Even to this day, America's most highly regarded literature tends to ring changes on the prodigal son or daughter motif, though there is seldom a forgiving parent at the end of the long journey into the self. The romance of Roanoke, then, seems to be but another American story centered upon our national fixation with disinheritance, a story with an especially frustrating irony at its core in that history, too, has contrived to deny us a secure family lineage. If Virginia Dare and the missing colonists are actually our spiritual ancestors, as national prophets-*cum*-historians like George Bancroft have informed us, then their disappearance is in some largely unacknowledged way an obstacle that we need to overcome in order to arrive at last at full self-knowledge and maturity. There is even— we might risk the conjecture—a degree of guilt in our curiosity, for we have not turned out to be the children of their empire, as we fancy they must have imagined us if they thought of us at all. Instead, we have sprung from rebellious children and have carved our own identities by rejecting the Elizabethan grace and monarchical majesty that our remote ancestors valued—in effect rejecting and abandoning them as well and thus, like Ann Landers's obsessed adolescent, sharing imaginatively and to some degree in the guilt of those Englishmen, four centuries gone, who did not return as they had promised because they had other things to do.

As with the culture, so with its constituency. Mary Virginia Wall's novel is affectionately dedicated to "Virginia, my Mother, and England, my Grandmother." In *Daughter of the Blood,* Herbert Bouldin Hawes brings the personal element of the quest still closer to the surface when he has his hero, Skah, try to allay Nonya-Virginia's anxieties about her own past with this address: "Thou wouldst know what happened at Ro-ano-ack on that terrible night, when thou wert not yet two years old. Thou canst not, of course, remember, e'en though I have told the tale of it. . . . 'Tis too far in the past. But methinks the record is writ in thy mind. . . ." The legend of the Lost Colony, it may be, compels our attention because it speaks in symbolic language of those remote periods in our own short span of years, possibly the preconscious life in the womb and almost certainly of our own lost memories of those first years of infancy.

The record, Freud and others have assured us, is indeed writ in our minds; but somehow we cannot make sense of it. The powerful appeal of most stories of lost things, in short—and this includes lost treasures and gold mines, lost chords, lost cities and civilizations, and missing links of every description—seems to originate in an urgent psychic need to fill in a hiatus in the soul's history and emerge from the quest a complete and continuous identity. To decipher these cryptic messages, to recover those lost talismanic treasures, to find again those missing people—that would be to discover a missing part of ourselves, to explore the deepest, most elusive recesses of our own unconscious minds and bring the sources of our being all the way up to a level of full awareness. "If you went over the mountain with me to the valley . . ." where the horstels (science-fiction versions of the Indians) live, says the horstel R'li (pronounced "really") in Philip José Farmer's *Dare*, "You'd become . . . [a] complete man. You'd become more balanced, more psychically integrated. The unconscious part of you would work hand in hand with the conscious. You'd not be chaotic, childish, out of tune." Perhaps the supreme act of psychic integration, our journey back toward our beginnings promises nothing less than the healing of all tragic inner division, the rediscovery of a primal language of pure symbol and dream; and if those goals seem by their very nature hopelessly out of reach, that is still no reason for not pursuing them with all the imaginative energy we can command.

Once we have begun to think in terms of archetypes, the rest is relatively easy. The story of the Lost Colony still holds our attention because, though we have from time to time employed it as a metaphor to comment on American politics and problems, it is actually a tale far older than America, the kind of fiction that many nations have found occasion to invent about themselves. In the *Aeneid*, for instance, Virgil bestowed upon Augustan Romans an ancestry that included, among other adventurers, a lost colony on the island of Crete, and Roman genealogy as he worked it out involved an intermixture of Trojan and Latin blood that must have seemed to Roanoke romancers an ideal poetic type of the fate they imagined for Ralegh's missing settlers.

Medieval and Renaissance Englishmen traced their lineage back to the dispossessed and widely wandering Brutus and from him to the legendary King Arthur, whose birthplace at Lyonesse, at least ac-

46

cording to the historian William Camden, was by the year 1600 a land as lost as Arthur's kingdom of Camelot had become. This list of vanished ancestors could, of course, be greatly extended, but the lure of the legend remains the same in virtually every known version: like stories of lost things in general, it appeals to our perplexity about the mysteries of our own generation and, additionally for Americans, provides a link with Western civilization through a shared imaginative heritage. Unique only on the surface, our myths and legends are really versions of immemorial stories that other people have told in other forms and fashions before America was discovered.

Still more striking than these general resemblances are the specific connections established between the Lost Colony and certain other legendary races whose history, so far as it is known, chronicles the disastrous consequences of some fatal flaw and, through the power of allusion, invests the story of Roanoke with an atmosphere of foreboding and guilt that affects the outcome of even the most enthusiastic celebrations of American progress. There is some curse, we seem to feel, entailed upon us by these ancestors we cannot ever know, some American sin that has not yet been expiated and perhaps never will be entirely; and it makes its power felt in tale after tale through all the imagery of blighted lands, strange transformations, wounds, warfare, and disease. As long ago as 1887 the poet Margaret Junkin Preston, sister-in-law of no less a southern hero than Stonewall Jackson, sensed this dimension of the saga; and in her poem "Croatan" she hinted at the true antiquity of the tale when she pondered the possibility that winter's icy ocean might have rolled inland "And overwhelmed the island's breadth, / And swept them all away."

Closer to our own time, two frustrated historians, reluctantly conceding that the fate of Roanoke would probably remain a mystery forever, lent at least tacit support to Preston's inspired guess. "If the whole island had sunk beneath the sea," they said, "this colony could not have been more completely lost to human sight and ken." What they are talking about, of course, is an American Atlantis, Plato's mythical island kingdom long associated with America in other contexts, which fell under divine interdiction and disappeared beneath the waters as punishment for the sin of pride. Once the very paradigm of power and ancient grace, this great civilization had long since vanished, even by Plato's time, and left, except for scattered traditions that kept its memory alive, not a wrack behind.

Nor is it difficult to identify the comparable sin of overweening arrogance that beset the inhabitants of the Lost Colony and, at least according to one pattern of mythic thinking, accounts for their disappearance to this very day: it is the sin of racial pride, of first and somehow final betrayal of the dream of brotherhood in a brave New World; and Virginia Dare herself is its most articulate spokesman. Indeed, in Cornelia Tuthill's prototypical tale, Virginia refused to wed Arcana because, as she confides to her mother, "He is an Indian, and I am an English woman." And although Eleanor Dare immediately protests against that sentiment, Virginia's statement would nonetheless be reported, in one fashion or another, by countless other maidens bearing her name before the tale of the Lost Colony ever reached the twentieth century.

Shallowly submerged below both the attractive sentimentality of Virginia's truncated affairs with innumerable Indian lovers and the Edenic imagery that normally accompanies the story, in other words, lurks an ancient tale of arrogance that tears the romance apart as a simple fantasy of retreat from the complexity of history toward a world of primal innocence and leaves Americans, every time they try to tell it, right back where they began: as lost amid the conflicting claims of our racial heritage, with vapid sentimentality on the one hand and brutal extermination on the other, as ever the Lost Colony was on the edge of an American wilderness. Another way to put the problem might be to suggest that we have told the tale so often because we have been telling it all wrong from the beginning and have yet to make it come out as, at some level of our awareness of what being American might have meant, we would wish to make it end. There is, perhaps, a world we can imagine but have not anywhere ever seen, a world beyond the bounds of time and history, where Virginia Dare and Arcana might be permitted to become the lovers of our fantasies without being touched by our most deeply felt sexual and racial taboos—but Roanoke, for all our efforts to restore its prelapsarian purity, is emphatically not that place.

Other versions of the archetype work toward similar thematic implications, with the possible exception of Stephen Vincent Benét's remark in *Western Star* (1943) that Ralegh's colonists had vanished in the American forest like the heroes of some "wild Irish tale"— Ossian, perhaps, who elected the apparent immortality of fairylands forlorn over his own human race and culture but lived to regret it, returning at last to a world completely out of kilter and aged beyond all expectation. More directly related to the motif of some inexpiable sin is the story of the Ten Lost Tribes of Israel, which at the very outset of Hebrew history went whoring after strange gods and, missing the chance to contribute to the building of the Jewish nation, thereafter were lost to God and human history—assimilated, exactly like the Roanoke settlers, into heathen tribes.

If this mythic parallel indicates another reason why Americans have found it difficult to forget about the Lost Colony—the more so because we have long associated ourselves with Biblical Israel as a people especially marked out for divine attention—it also seems to reverse the meanings of the Atlantis allusion, bringing us back to the condemnatory tones of John Lawson's *New Voyage* by intimating that the missing colonists, like the Ten Lost Tribes, richly deserve their fate for their betrayal of religion, race, and culture. The burden of guilt remains squarely on the colonists' shoulders, but now the mythic substructure of the story serves to focus the ambivalence that Americans seem always to have felt—regardless of how any given era in our history may have placed its emphasis—when confronting the complex issues of savagery versus civilization, pastoralism versus progress, and the simple equality of natural law versus the unavoidable complications and hierarchies that attend advanced social systems.

And there is yet another mythic element in the story, this one intimately related to the tale of the Ten Lost Tribes. Urged relentlessly onward for century after century, drifting as in Edison Marshall's *Lost Colony* from tribe to tribe without finding a permanent place of refuge, Ralegh's settlers remind us inevitably of the Wandering Jew, cursed by Christ and doomed to wander throughout history without either home or homeland until the final trumpet sounds. The oral tradition of the returning ship, which calls to mind the *Flying Dutchman* and other similar stories, testifies to the fact that the folk imagination saw this connection in some dim way also. Throughout most Roanoke fiction, at any rate, the idea of endless wandering runs as a strong thematic undercurrent; and sometimes, as in Clifford Wayne Hartridge's *Manteo,* it breaks through to the surface. "Somewhere in that great unknown country," Hartridge's hero reflects, a good fictional century and a quarter after the fact, "the wandering descendants of the exiles from the Island of Roanoke were finding refuge.

How far would they have to travel, through what dangerous tribes would they pass, as generation after generation they journeyed, perhaps without even the old Israel's hope of ultimately finding a promised land?" It is an awesome price to pay for any transgression, this permanent dislocation from all history and deliberate destination, and we feel pity and terror in the presence of such hopeless wayfarers.

And we feel, perhaps, the stirrings of these tragic emotions not only for the sake of those wandering outcasts, truly people without a country, but also for ourselves, restless Americans on an endless diaspora, whose very history, which should at least confirm our habitation and our name, confirms instead our essential rootlessness. In granting us the Lost Colony, in any event, history seems to have helped us to a particularly fortuitous symbol of the consequences of our own polyglot identities—part English, part white American, part Indian, and God knows what all else—a problem of self-definition that surely plays a part in our historic wanderings as a nation. More than that, it is the peculiar curse of the religion of progress to which most Americans remain devoted that we are ever marching onward, never perfect or historically fulfilled at any moment. The best we are now, our American faith informs us, will be improved upon by those who follow after—and by their sons the same after them. Like the Roanoke colonists, we tramp a perpetual journey; and Ralegh's forlorn settlers move us across the centuries as a striking image of man alone in time, incomplete and imperfect—a picture that possesses even greater force for us because these aliens, lacking a coherent history and unable to participate in the promise of the future, seem so much like ourselves.

As it happens, in fact, our American diaspora may even have its sources in the same historical crime of which the Roanoke colonists stand accused. At least one commentator on the American scene, the English novelist D. H. Lawrence, thought so at any rate, and in his *Studies in Classic American Literature* he sought to explain the origins of what he called "the great American grouch, the Orestes-like frenzy of restlessness in the Yankee soul" by reference to the white man's extirpation of the Indians. "[W]ithin the present generation," Lawrence wrote in 1923, the same year in which Mary Johnston's *Croatan* was published, "the surviving Red Indians are due to merge in the great white swamp. Then the Daimon of America will work

50

overtly. . . ." If the Roanoke novels are any evidence, Lawrence's prophecy would seem to have been at least partially fulfilled in the drastic shift in the treatment of Virginia Dare and the stress upon primitivism that mark the romance after 1930 or so.

But it is somewhat curious that Lawrence, uncommonly sensitive to the psychological tensions that arise from being both sons and lovers at the same time, was not alert to still another potential source of American frenzy—the adolescent ambivalence toward women born of the revolt against the domineering mother, which has been part of America's buried psychic life at least since the days of the Revolution. Certainly, an even greater crime than genocide lurks in Lawrence's allusions to Orestes; and since we have as well the explicit reference in Edison Marshall's *Lost Colony* to a crime committed by an anonymous colonist who might have provoked the Furies from their "foul nests," we may be justified in following Lawrence's remarks in a direction that he apparently did not intend.

That direction, of course, leads us right to Virginia Dare, the saintly and yet strangely sensuous heroine who has come down to us in several avatars. As the infant of Roanoke, she lends her prestige to the theme of divinely appointed destiny, the unstoppable spread of Christian civilization across the heathen continent. Herbert Bouldin Hawes brings Virginia and the Lost Colony together for this symbolic purpose when he reminds us that Roanoke was "England's first born by savage America"—mysteriously stillborn, as things turned out— but with its death it purchased renewed life for man and "the dawn of a new day for the world." Exactly how this colonial failure produced such grandly messianic results Hawes neglects to tell us; but we may surmise from Sallie Southall Cotten's description of Eleanor and Virginia as "Mother and child, as in Bethlehem story" or, for that matter, from the "Adoration of Childhood" sequence in Paul Green's *Lost Colony*, a scene complete with angelic voices offstage and a halo of virginal blue-and-white light, that it had something to do with the rescue of Old Adam from the wilderness of European corruption by a youthful savior who brings innocence, light, and life into a world darkly stained by the crimes of history but whose promise of progress, alas, involves a reenactment of the same crimes in a New World context and the sacrifice of a spotless babe to set things right again. If only it had been that simple.

In this scene from Paul Green's outdoor drama *The Lost Colony* Eleanor Dare (played by Marjalene Thomas), holding her baby, Virginia, looks toward the sea for the help from England that never came. Photograph from Paul Green, *The Lost Colony: A Symphonic Drama of Man's Faith and Work* (Durham: Seeman Printery, Four Hundredth Anniversary Edition, 1980), following p. 75.

The patron saint of Manifest Destiny, Virginia Dare also turns easily into a Protestant Madonna (despite the small problem of her virginal status) from whose womb there sprung by some sort of inexplicable ethnogenesis a race of heroes unknown before in history. Proficient with bow and arrow, able to converse in the language of a multitude of wild beasts, she also anachronistically yearns to read *Hamlet* and exerts a pervasive moral influence over the savage pagans, two very different kinds of accomplishments that suggest that in her, Americans find a symbol of accommodation and transformation, an acknowledgment that the wildness in American blood has indeed been tempered by the best of European virtues. She might, in fact, serve this purpose far better than her putative daughter Pocahontas, were it not that her offspring must perforce be more savage than civilized. Thus the ritualistic rejections of the dark, sensual self that allures even as it distresses her, the nearly endless succession of impossible white lovers, the Christian marriages arranged in absolute despair by writers like E. A. B. Shackelford.

The hot blood will burn in an Indian wilderness no less than in the streets of London, something that is perhaps intimated at some level by Virginia's transformation into an animal: a clever way of preserving her purity for symbolic and deadly penetration while punishing her for having so much as entertained the idea of an Indian lover. Sentimentalize her how they will, most Roanoke romancers feel some ambivalence about Virginia at her best—while at her worst she inspires outright hostility for her betrayal of her culture and of the purity of her gender—and so they change her into a doe whose very color mocks her failure to remain unsullied in her heart and symbolically expresses her sexual degeneration and racial transgression.

As the mythic progenitress of American culture, then, Virginia Dare has proved something of an embarrassment to American authors, while as an object of our adolescent sexual fantasies, a virginal maiden who is nonetheless associated with the tawny Indian lasses who decorate the setting of her tale, she is even more troublesome to deal with. For although she is clearly an alluring figure—the all-American girl dressed up in revealingly scanty doeskins—in another way she is a forbidding, threatening goddess who carries the emblems of her asexual power in her hands, combining the roles of virgin huntress and mother-conscience in her ability to mete out punishment and prohibit us from peering too closely at the mysteries of our own generation.

Suppose we should turn down some dark and tangled forest path and come upon the very deed itself, stripped of all poetry and senti-ment and revealed as nothing more than passionate lovemaking with some dusky savage? This, or something very much like it, is what happens to the hero of Edison Marshall's *Lost Colony* just before he slays the druidic priestess Winifred in an act that symbolically con-firms the earlier charge that he had murdered his mother; and it is an experience that seems to await virtually every author who has ever picked up a pen to attempt to tell Virginia's story. Among other things, it suggests that part of the prohibitive power with which Virginia has been endowed in her avatar as Artemis is deliberately bestowed upon her in covert acknowledgment that what she can tell us we do not really want to know, that the price of such knowledge might be the destruction of our own most cherished illusions of charity and motherhood.

Deeply embedded in the Roanoke romance, in other words, is the myth of Diana and Acteon, a mythic tableau portraying sexual anx-iety, flight and pursuit, and the inevitable consequences of probing too insistently into the secrets of procreation; so that while Virginia does indeed tempt us—only think of the knowledge she could share!—we nevertheless approach her image hesitantly, not as ardent lovers but in fear and trembling, like curious little boys intuitively certain that the sight they might see will not be worth the disillusionment. Given the choice, we shy from that moment of full and final discovery, of enforced recognition that our mythic mother is in all ways the same as those libidinous Indian maidens upon whom we project all our fears of her suspected sensuality. Even more than the historical hiatus itself, this psychological tactic, perhaps a necessary one if the demands of a national mythology consistent with our cultural evasions of sexuality are to be met, accounts for the peculiarly truncated quality that afflicts even the longest of the Roanoke romances.

Still, all prohibition and no play makes Virginia a very dull girl indeed. Twentieth-century writers, in any case, have come to feel far more comfortable with the soft, yielding, and yet somehow forbidden Indian maidens whom she attempts to displace in their affections, usually with just enough success to make modern heroes feel guilty about sexual self-indulgence also. Cast in this role, in short, Virginia is but another name for the sexless, emasculating women who populate so much other American fiction—the parallels with James's Isabel Archer, another American Diana, are indeed compelling—and whom we pretend to desire while our hearts (and other, still more private parts of our anatomy as well) are yearning for the dark temptress of our secret dreams. At this level, then, Virginia Dare may satisfy our sense of propriety and piety, but we are content to feel somewhat free of her at last and, when we permit ourselves to think about her at all, probably wish that she would stay lost forever. If, at another level, we find ourselves unable to let this take place as we ought to, it is probably because, though we have grown to dislike her more and more, we have yet to make up our minds absolutely about whether the civilization she symbolizes might not, after all, be worth its discontents.

The romance of Roanoke is, then, one of the richest and most provocative stories of its kind in American literature. The fact that no really first-rate storyteller has yet been attracted to it—which might at first seem an insurmountable obstacle to its continued longevity—proves in the end to be still another reason why it is important to Americans, for if, as Richard Chase informed us some twenty years ago, the American novel characteristically rests in and sustains the fundamental contradictions of our culture, then the tale of Ralegh's Lost Colonists, precisely the sort of historical romance that Chase would dismiss as too trivial for serious consideration, provides persuasive evidence that both our popular and serious fictions originate in similar contradictory impulses and in ambivalent attitudes toward the American past and the meaning of America. Or we may, if we wish, argue instead that the Roanoke romance helps to confirm Daniel Hoffman's thesis that most important American stories derive both theme and structure from underlying ancient fables. Either way, the story of the Lost Colony and Virginia Dare, badly told though it may be in individual instances, collectively demonstrates that even relatively insignificant American writers may make major contributions to the American literary tradition and that a culture may be comprehended almost equally well by its most adolescent fantasies as by its most high-minded and sophisticated fictions. Ralegh's missing settlers still haunt the American imagination not simply because history, like nature, abhors a vacuum but also because they have not yet imparted all the wisdom that such wayward wanderers may be presumed to possess.